# THE MAZE CRAZE

## BY SALLY STONE

Learning Media®

# CONTENTS

# 1. MANY MAZES

A maze is a place that has many paths
that join together and twist and turn.
Each path looks the same, but some
have dead ends! There's usually only
one way into a maze and one way out.
The **challenge** is to find your way to
the end.

There are many different kinds of mazes. You may have done a maze on paper or found your way through a mirror maze at a fun park.

Maybe you've even been inside a maze that's made from plants, such as a **hedge** maze or a **maize** maze.

Mazes can also be made from stone or wood. There are even mazes that are made using water!

# 2. THE MINOTAUR MAZE

The oldest maze we know of is in a Greek story. This story tells of a king who owned a dangerous animal called a minotaur. The animal had the head of a bull and the body of a man. It lived in a maze.

The king was the ruler of Crete, an island near Greece. In Greece, there was another king who ruled a city called Athens.

Once every nine years, the King of
Crete ordered the King of Athens to
send seven young men and seven
young women for the minotaur to eat.
The King of Athens was scared of the
King of Crete and his army, so he did
as he was told.

The King of Athens had a son named Theseus. One day, Theseus said that he would go kill the minotaur.

Theseus took a ball of string into the maze so that he would know where he'd been. He tied the string to the door of the maze and let it out behind him.

Theseus walked through the maze until
he found a large, dark cave. The minotaur
was inside. Theseus killed the minotaur and
followed the string back out of the maze.

Today, there is a place in Greece where you can see there was once a maze. Some people think this is a copy of where the minotaur lived.

# 3. HEDGE MAZES

Usually, people go into a maze to have fun!

Hedge mazes were first built for royal families. They were later built in parks and other places so that everyone could enjoy them.

One of the most famous hedge mazes is at Hampton Court Palace, which is in England. This maze was planted in the 1690s for the King of England.

Hampton Court Palace

The paths in the Hampton Court maze are half a mile (almost a kilometer) long. It takes about twenty minutes to walk to the center.

Try to find your way to the middle. It may look simple, but it's easy to get lost!

Turn to page 30 for the answer.

The largest hedge maze in the world is in Hawaii. It's around seven times bigger than the Hampton Court maze.

# 4. MIRROR MAZES

Mirror mazes are often small. However, when you walk through a mirror maze, it looks six times larger than it really is!

This is because most of what you see are **reflections**. It looks as if there are many paths around you, but most of them are mirrors.

Sometimes, a mirror maze has lights and sounds. These can make the reflections seem more real. It's very easy to get lost in a mirror maze!

When astronauts are training to go into space, they use small mirror mazes to practice finding their way. This helps them figure out what's going on around them when they're in a strange place.

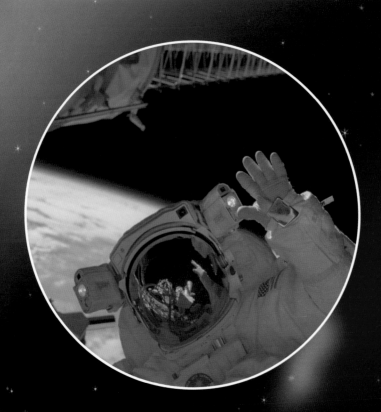

# 5. MAIZE MAZES

In many places, farmers are letting people make maize mazes on their farms.

The first maize maze was built in 1993. It was thought of by a famous maze maker named Adrian Fisher.

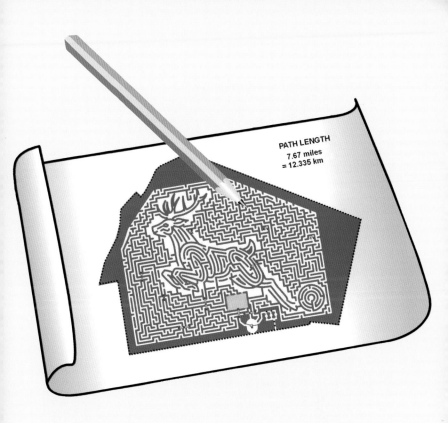

PATH LENGTH
7.67 miles
= 12.335 km

People who make maize mazes cut huge shapes through the fields. It can take weeks for them to plan and cut the mazes.

When a maize maze is finished, people pay the farmer to go inside. They might take most of the day to find their way to the end of the maze.

Each maize maze is used for part of a summer, and then the maize is cut. The maize is then used for food.

Many states in America have maize mazes cut in a shape that tells people something about the state. In California, a maze was cut in the shape of the star and bear that are on the state flag.

Some maize mazes are so big that people are given a map to help them know where to go. Many mazes also have people who will find you if you get lost.

Tip: If you burn in the sun, always wear sunblock and a hat as you walk around. It can be hot work finding your way through a maze!

Today, more mazes are being built than ever before. They come in all shapes and sizes, and they are made from different things. The maze craze is here to stay!

# Answer to the Hampton Court maze

# GLOSSARY

(These words are printed in bold type
the first time they appear in the book.)

**challenge**: something that is difficult
to do

**hedge**: a wall made by bushes
growing close together

**maize**: a tall grass that is grown for
food (also called corn)

**reflection**: the copy of something that
you see in a mirror

# INDEX